THINK INSTEAD

*Daily Affirmations for
Women Healing Through Anger*

By
Lynnette C. Anderson

Copyright © 2025 by Lynnette C. Anderson

CONTENTS

Dedication 5

Acknowledgments 6

MONTH 1: LIFE 7

MONTH 2: LOVE 17

MONTH 3: AWARENESS 26

MONTH 4: ACKNOWLEDGMENT 36

MONTH 5: ACCEPTANCE 46

MONTH 6: FORGIVENESS 56

MONTH 7: UNDERSTANDING 66

MONTH 8: FAITH 76

MONTH 9: TRUST 86

MONTH 10: WORTH 96

MONTH 11: SERVICE 106

MONTH 12: PEACE 116

About the Author 126

DEDICATION

To my mother, Anita G. Anderson—

Thank you for teaching me what resilience looks like, what love feels like, and what healing requires. Your strength shaped my own, and your wisdom lives on in every word I write.

ACKNOWLEDGMENTS

To the women in *Think Instead: Daily Affirmations for Women Healing Through Anger*— This work exists because of your stories, your silence, your breakthroughs, and your brave beginnings. Thank you for showing that anger, when met with intention, becomes a source of deep power, lasting purpose, and real peace.

To every woman who has ever been told to 'calm down' when her anger was actually a cry for connection—I see you.

This book is for the ones who carry their fire and their softness in the same body. For the women breaking cycles, learning emotional intelligence, and choosing to heal out loud.

Thank you to my clients, sisters, daughters, aunties, mothers, and mentors who remind me daily of the power and beauty in feeling deeply.

To the women reading this: may you think instead—before reacting, before abandoning yourself, before giving away your peace.

You are powerful. You are healing. You are whole.

MONTH 1:
LIFE

You Are Still Here—And That Matters.

This month is about honoring your breath, your story, and your survival. Every step forward is sacred ground.

WEEK 1: January 1–7

Day 1

Affirmation: I am alive, and that is enough for today.

How to Implement: Place your hand on your heart and feel your breath.

There was a day I barely made it out of bed. I didn't brush my hair or check my phone. I just lay there wondering if anything I did even mattered. But then I placed my hand on my chest and felt my heart thudding. That small, steady beat reminded me—I'm still here. Maybe that's all I needed to do that day. And that was enough.

Day 2

Affirmation: I give myself permission to begin again.

How to Implement: Start over today. No apology needed.

I snapped at someone I loved—again. The guilt hit instantly, and for a while, I thought I'd ruined everything. But instead of spiraling, I paused, took a breath, and said, 'Can I try again?' To my surprise, they smiled and said yes. That moment taught me that life gives us new chances if we're humble enough to take them.

Day 3

Affirmation: Every breath is proof that I can keep going.

How to Implement: Inhale for 4 counts. Hold. Exhale for 4. Repeat 3 times.

I once had a panic attack in a grocery store aisle. My chest tightened, and I thought I might pass out. I dropped everything and focused on my breath. Just in, out, in, out. When it passed, I didn't feel embarrassed—I felt victorious. Breathing got me through. It always has.

Day 4

Affirmation: I am learning how to live, not just survive.

How to Implement: Do one thing today that brings you joy, not just relief.

I used to move through my days like a checklist—wake up, work, sleep. One day, I sat in the sun for no reason at all. I watched clouds float by like slow-moving ships. That tiny moment wasn't productive, but it felt alive. That's when I realized joy doesn't ask for permission. It asks for presence.

Day 5

Affirmation: I am not behind. I am on my own timeline.

How to Implement: Say no to comparison today.

Everyone around me seemed to be winning—new jobs, marriages, babies, houses. I was just trying to keep my plants alive. But one evening, my friend said, 'You're growing too—just differently.' That stuck with me. Life isn't a race. It's a rhythm.

Day 6

Affirmation: Life itself is a miracle worth honoring.

How to Implement: Notice something beautiful today—something simple and alive.

There was a morning when I was rushing so fast, I nearly missed the sunrise. I stopped at a red light and just stared at the sky, painted in soft purples and golds. That moment reminded me that life is still happening, whether I slow down for it or not.

Day 7

Affirmation: My presence matters more than my perfection.

How to Implement: Take one mindful breath before you respond to anything today.

I used to rush to fix everything—to be everything. But on Day 7, I paused. I showed up fully, not flawlessly. And someone said, 'Thank you for just being here.' That's when I realized my presence was enough, even when I didn't have the answers.

WEEK 2: January 8–14

Day 8

Affirmation: I honor my growth, even when it's messy.

How to Implement: Reflect on one way you've grown this month.

There was a time I thought growth had to look graceful. But when I lost my temper and apologized without justifying it, that was growth too. It was messy, real, and mine.

Day 9

Affirmation: I deserve joy without guilt.

How to Implement: Do something fun today—just because.

I used to think I had to earn joy by being productive. Then one afternoon I danced in my kitchen to an old song, and laughed until I cried. That joy reminded me I'm allowed to feel light.

Day 10

Affirmation: I can slow down without falling behind.

How to Implement: Take a five-minute pause today—no agenda.

One day I sat in the car after work and did nothing. Just breathed. That tiny moment of stillness didn't solve anything—but it gave me the strength to face everything.

Day 11

Affirmation: I release the pressure to be perfect.

How to Implement: Make one mistake today—and don't fix it.

I burned dinner and started to apologize. But then I said, 'It's fine, let's eat it anyway.' We laughed. It wasn't perfect, but it was real. And that was enough.

Day 12

Affirmation: I am healing at my own pace.

How to Implement: Say out loud, 'I am not in a race.'

When I compared my healing to others, I felt behind. But when I looked back at how far I'd come, I realized I wasn't stuck—I was rebuilding. Quietly. Powerfully.

Day 13

Affirmation: I trust myself to handle what comes.

How to Implement: Recall one hard thing you've overcome.

I didn't think I could handle the breakup, but I did. I cried, journaled, prayed, and got through it. That memory reminds me: I can trust me.

Day 14

Affirmation: I let go of what I can't control.

How to Implement: List one thing today that's not your job to fix.

I used to carry everyone's emotions like they were mine. But I'm learning that love doesn't mean rescuing. It means standing beside someone, not saving them.

WEEK 3: January 15–21

Day 15

Affirmation: I speak to myself with kindness.

How to Implement: Replace one self-criticism today with compassion.

I caught myself saying, 'You're so stupid.' Then I paused and said, 'You made a mistake, and you're learning.' That small shift softened my whole day.

Day 16

Affirmation: I am allowed to rest without guilt.

How to Implement: Take a 10-minute break today and just breathe.

I used to push through exhaustion until I snapped. One afternoon, I lay down for 15 minutes. The world didn't fall apart—but I started to feel whole again.

Day 17

Affirmation: My feelings are valid, even if others don't understand them.

How to Implement: Name what you're feeling today—without explaining it away.

Someone told me to 'calm down' when I cried. I almost apologized. But instead, I said, 'I'm allowed to feel this.' And I stood in that truth.

Day 18

Affirmation: I am not my worst moment.

How to Implement: Think of one time you forgave someone. Offer the same grace to yourself.

I remembered something I did years ago that still stings. But then I thought of a friend who forgave me without hesitation. If she could, maybe I can too.

Day 19

Affirmation: I welcome peace, even when chaos is near.

How to Implement: Light a candle or find a small quiet space today.

The house was loud and messy. I lit a candle, sat on the floor, and breathed. I didn't escape the chaos, but I found peace inside it.

Day 20

Affirmation: I can be soft and strong at the same time.

How to Implement: Show love to someone today without losing yourself.

I said 'no' with a gentle voice. They were surprised—but they respected it. That's when I realized boundaries are love too.

Day 21

Affirmation: I am not responsible for other people's happiness.

How to Implement: Let someone feel what they feel—without trying to fix it.

My friend was sad, and I rushed to cheer her up. But she said, 'I just need you to listen.' That day I learned presence is more powerful than fixing.

WEEK 4: January 22–28

Day 22

Affirmation: I release the need to prove myself.

How to Implement: Notice when you're trying to earn approval—then pause.

I caught myself overexplaining something at work, hoping to sound smart. Then I stopped, took a breath, and said, 'That's enough.' I realized I don't need to prove my worth—it's already there.

Day 23

Affirmation: I can begin again, even in the middle of the mess.

How to Implement: Choose one thing to reset today—a thought, a space, or a conversation.

My day started with chaos—spilled coffee, a harsh text, tears. But instead of calling it ruined, I stepped outside, breathed, and said, 'I'm starting over.' That moment became the turning point.

Day 24

Affirmation: I do not shrink to make others comfortable.

How to Implement: Speak one truth today that you normally hide.

I used to laugh off comments that hurt. One day, I said, 'That wasn't okay with me.' It was awkward—but honest. And afterward, I felt taller.

Day 25

Affirmation: I am allowed to take up space.

How to Implement: Stand tall today. Literally. Roll your shoulders back and breathe deep.

At a meeting, I almost skipped sharing my idea. But I raised my hand. My voice shook—but I spoke. And when someone nodded in agreement, I remembered that my voice matters.

Day 26

Affirmation: I trust the woman I'm becoming.

How to Implement: Write a note to your future self today.

I used to second-guess everything. One day, I wrote a letter that said, 'Keep going. You're doing better than you think.' Rereading it weeks later gave me strength I didn't know I'd need.

Day 27

Affirmation: I can be proud without being perfect.

How to Implement: Celebrate something small you accomplished today.

I finally organized that drawer I'd been avoiding. It wasn't a big deal to anyone else—but to me, it felt like momentum. Progress, not perfection.

Day 28

Affirmation: My boundaries are a form of self-respect.

How to Implement: Say 'no' to something today without apologizing.

Someone asked for a favor I didn't have capacity for. I said, 'No, I can't today.' They understood. And I felt peace instead of guilt—for the first time in a long time.

MONTH 2:

LOVE

Love Begins With How You Speak To Yourself.

This month, we turn inward to rewrite the stories that told us we were unworthy. You are not just lovable—you are love.

WEEK 1: February 1–7

Day 1

Affirmation: I am worthy of love without conditions.

How to Implement: Say 'I am lovable as I am' in the mirror today.

For years, I thought I had to be perfect to deserve love. Then someone hugged me while I was falling apart and whispered, 'You're still enough.' That's when I started to believe it.

Day 2

Affirmation: I give love to myself without shame.

How to Implement: Treat yourself the way you wish others would.

One Valentine's Day, I bought myself flowers. Not out of loneliness—but celebration. It felt awkward at first, but then I smiled. I realized I could be my own reason to feel adored.

Day 3

Affirmation: I do not beg for what should be freely given.

How to Implement: Let go of someone or something that makes you feel unworthy.

I kept texting someone who left me on read. Every message chipped at my dignity. One day, I deleted the thread and said, 'No more chasing.' That silence felt like power.

Day 4

Affirmation: I can love and let go at the same time.

How to Implement: Write a goodbye note to something you've outgrown.

There was a relationship I held onto long past its expiration. I finally let it go—not because I stopped caring, but because I started caring for myself more.

Day 5

Affirmation: I am learning to receive love, not just give it.

How to Implement: Say 'thank you' without deflecting next time someone compliments you.

When someone said, 'You're amazing,' I used to laugh it off. Then one day, I just said, 'Thank you.' That moment cracked open a door to self-acceptance.

Day 6

Affirmation: I do not confuse pain with love.

How to Implement: Notice one red flag you've normalized—and name it.

I thought love meant sacrifice. But after years of walking on eggshells, I realized: love shouldn't hurt. Respect doesn't need to be earned through suffering.

Day 7

Affirmation: My love is valuable, and I choose who receives it.

How to Implement: Make a list of people who nourish your spirit—and one boundary to protect your peace.

I used to give my love to anyone who asked. Now I pause and ask, 'Are they safe with my heart?' That question saved me from a lot of regret.

WEEK 2: February 8–14

Day 8

Affirmation: I no longer abandon myself to be loved by others.

How to Implement: Notice one time today when you silence your needs—then speak them instead.

I used to nod and say 'I'm fine' when I wasn't. One day, I said, 'Actually, I'm not okay.' That truth felt like love—a love I gave to myself first.

Day 9

Affirmation: I choose relationships that feel safe, not just familiar.

How to Implement: Journal about one trait that makes you feel emotionally safe.

He reminded me of someone from my past—charming but unpredictable. I realized I was chasing a pattern, not peace. That day, I chose different.

Day 10

Affirmation: I am not hard to love—I've just accepted less than I deserve.

How to Implement: Repeat this: 'I am not too much. I am not too little. I am enough.'

Someone once told me I was 'too emotional.' For years, I believed them. Then I met someone who said, 'I love how deeply you feel.' That changed everything.

Day 11

Affirmation: I let love find me while I'm busy loving myself.

How to Implement: Do one thing today that's purely for your own joy.

I stopped swiping and started painting again. That day, I smiled more than I had in weeks. Love didn't text me—but I felt full anyway.

Day 12

Affirmation: I no longer confuse being needed with being loved.

How to Implement: Ask yourself, 'Do I feel chosen—or just useful?'

They always called when they were in crisis. I always answered. One day, I let it ring. That silence taught me the difference between being loved and being used.

Day 13

Affirmation: I am learning to stay when love is good.

How to Implement: Notice when you want to sabotage something safe—and choose presence instead.

He was kind. Consistent. No games. I almost ran. But I stayed. That choice felt unfamiliar—but healing often does.

Day 14

Affirmation: I am my own Valentine.

How to Implement: Celebrate yourself today—out loud, in writing, or in action.

One February 14th, I set the table for one. Candles. Music. My favorite meal. I toasted to my own heart—and it was the most romantic night I've had.

WEEK 3: February 15–21

Day 15

Affirmation: I no longer love people at the expense of myself.

How to Implement: Check in: Are you caring or self-sacrificing? Choose balance.

I stayed up all night helping him through his mess, even though I had nothing left to give. Now, I ask myself, 'Can I show up without abandoning me?' That check-in saves me.

Day 16

Affirmation: I choose partners who respect my silence as much as my words.

How to Implement: Spend quiet time with someone and notice how they hold space for you.

He didn't interrupt when I didn't speak. He just held my hand. That moment made me feel more seen than any compliment ever had.

Day 17

Affirmation: I no longer confuse attachment with affection.

How to Implement: Ask: 'Am I holding on to love or just afraid to be alone?'

The texts, the drama, the highs and lows—I thought that was passion. But when I stepped away and found peace, I realized it was chaos dressed as connection.

Day 18

Affirmation: I can be vulnerable without being weak.

How to Implement: Share one tender truth today—with yourself or someone safe.

I told her I missed her. No walls, no ego. Just truth. And instead of rejection, I felt closeness. That moment taught me that softness is strength.

Day 19

Affirmation: I am loving myself back to wholeness.

How to Implement: Write a list of things that make you feel deeply loved.

I lit incense, ran a bath, and said, 'This is for me.' It wasn't a special occasion—it was a Tuesday. But I felt seen by myself. That mattered.

Day 20

Affirmation: I attract what I believe I deserve.

How to Implement: Affirm: 'I am ready for healthy love.'

Once I stopped settling, everything shifted. The way I walked, spoke, and chose. My standards rose—and so did my peace.

Day 21

Affirmation: I let go of old versions of love that hurt me.

How to Implement: Bless and release one memory today—it doesn't define you.

I used to romanticize someone who never valued me. Now, I say thank you for the lesson—and close the door. Love shouldn't come with bruises.

WEEK 4: February 22–28

Day 22

Affirmation: I let love feel easy, not earned.

How to Implement: Receive kindness today without deflecting it.

She brought me coffee just because. My first instinct was to say, 'You didn't have to.' But then I smiled and said, 'Thank you.' Love isn't always grand—it's often quiet and kind.

Day 23

Affirmation: I am whole, even without a partner.

How to Implement: Celebrate one thing you love about being alone.

I used to dread empty weekends. Now, I use them to reconnect—with myself, my dreams, my peace. Solitude became sacred.

Day 24

Affirmation: I let love grow slowly and safely.

How to Implement: Pause before labeling a connection—just feel it.

We talked for weeks before even discussing 'us.' There was no rush. Just ease. That's when I realized: love that lasts isn't urgent—it's intentional.

Day 25

Affirmation: I do not settle for breadcrumbs when I deserve the feast.

How to Implement: Say no to halfway love today.

They texted 'miss you' at midnight. The old me would've replied instantly. This me didn't answer. I deserve consistent care—not crumbs.

Day 26

Affirmation: I trust love that doesn't confuse me.

How to Implement: Ask: Does this feel safe or just exciting?

There were no mixed signals. No guessing. Just truth. That quiet steadiness felt foreign—and beautiful.

Day 27

Affirmation: I choose love that adds peace, not chaos.

How to Implement: Reflect on what love has felt like when it was calm—and real.

He never raised his voice. Never disappeared. He showed up, again and again. Love, I learned, can feel like safety.

Day 28

Affirmation: I love myself enough to wait for love that loves me back.

How to Implement: Write a note to your future partner—one who meets you with care.

I used to fall for potential. Now, I wait for reciprocity. Not because I'm hard to please—but because I've finally learned what I'm worth.

MONTH 3:
AWARENESS

You Can't Heal What You Won't Face.

This month, we practice seeing clearly: our triggers, our strengths, and the emotions beneath the anger. Awareness is power.

WEEK 1: March 1–7

Day 1

Affirmation: I allow myself to see what I've been avoiding.

How to Implement: Gently name one truth you've been sidestepping.

I kept saying, 'I'm just tired,' when I was really burnt out. The day I admitted I was overwhelmed was the day I finally started asking for help.

Day 2

Affirmation: I can witness my emotions without drowning in them.

How to Implement: When a strong feeling shows up today, say: 'I see you.'

My anger used to scare me. But one afternoon, I sat with it instead of stuffing it. I asked it what it needed. It said, 'Rest.' That surprised me—and softened me.

Day 3

Affirmation: **Awareness is the beginning of healing.**

How to Implement: **Reflect on one pattern that keeps repeating in your life.**

I kept ending up in friendships where I felt invisible. The day I asked, 'What am I accepting that I shouldn't be?' was the day I began to choose differently.

Day 4

Affirmation: I honor my inner signals, even if others don't understand them.

How to Implement: Follow a gut feeling today—even if it seems inconvenient.

I canceled plans last-minute because something felt off. Later, I found out I avoided unnecessary drama. I've learned to trust my knowing.

Day 5

Affirmation: My thoughts are not facts—they are habits.

How to Implement: Write down one negative thought and respond to it with compassion.

The voice in my head said, 'You always mess up.' I wrote it down, then replied, 'Actually, I've grown. I just made a mistake.' It shifted everything.

Day 6

Affirmation: I don't have to understand everything to take the next step.

How to Implement: Take one small action today without overthinking it.

I didn't know how I'd fix the mess, but I cleaned one corner. That one step created momentum. Awareness made space for action.

Day 7

Affirmation: I pause before I react—and that is power.

How to Implement: Breathe before you respond to anything that triggers you today.

Someone said something rude, and I almost snapped. Instead, I took a breath and said, 'I need a minute.' That pause protected my peace—and my dignity.

WEEK 2: March 8–14

Day 8

Affirmation: I notice what I feel instead of judging it.

How to Implement: Pause and name your emotion today—without needing to change it.

I used to say, 'I shouldn't feel this way.' One day I just said, 'I'm disappointed.' No judgment. Just truth. That honesty felt like relief.

Day 9

Affirmation: I can hold two truths at once.

How to Implement: Acknowledge a moment today when joy and sorrow coexist.

I laughed while remembering someone I miss. The ache was still there—but so was gratitude. That's when I realized emotions can share space.

Day 10

Affirmation: Awareness brings clarity—not always comfort.

How to Implement: Sit with one uncomfortable truth today without reacting to it.

I realized I was the one ghosting healthy habits. It stung. But naming it gave me a starting point. Clarity became a compass.

Day 11

Affirmation: I am not afraid of my own depth.

How to Implement: Ask yourself: 'What am I feeling beneath the surface today?'

I felt irritated, but when I looked deeper, I found grief. The awareness didn't make it easier—but it made it make sense.

Day 12

Affirmation: I witness my patterns with compassion.

How to Implement: Notice a habit today without shame—just curiosity.

Every time I felt ignored, I shut down. One day I said, 'Oh, I do this because I used to feel invisible.' That awareness softened the edges of my defense.

Day 13

Affirmation: The more I see myself clearly, the more I heal.

How to Implement: Write one sentence that reflects how far you've come.

I used to avoid mirrors. Then one morning, I said, 'You've survived so much.' I didn't flinch. I smiled.

Day 14

Affirmation: I respond, not react—and that's growth.

How to Implement: Take a breath before responding to something hard today.

Someone criticized me unfairly. I wanted to snap back. Instead, I said, 'Thanks for the feedback.' Then I walked away. That was growth I could feel in my bones.

WEEK 3: March 15–21

Day 15

Affirmation: I notice when I'm triggered and pause with purpose.

How to Implement: When you feel activated today, ask: 'What's really going on beneath this?'

She said something that hit a nerve. I felt heat rise—but I paused. Underneath my anger was hurt. That pause helped me speak from the truth, not the wound.

Day 16

Affirmation: I am learning to see myself with gentle eyes.

How to Implement: Replace one self-criticism with kindness today.

I looked in the mirror and caught myself thinking, 'You look rough.' I stopped and said, 'You look like someone who's trying.' That felt softer, and true.

Day 17

Affirmation: I pay attention to what drains me and what fills me.

How to Implement: List one thing that energizes you and one thing that exhausts you.

After lunch with someone who only complains, I felt depleted. But a walk in silence refilled me. That contrast was the lesson.

Day 18

Affirmation: Awareness is a gift, even when it's uncomfortable.

How to Implement: **Name one hard truth you've outgrown the need to avoid.**

I finally admitted I stayed in that friendship out of fear of being alone. That truth hurt—but it set me free.

Day 19

Affirmation: I honor what my body is trying to tell me.

How to Implement: **Tune in today—where in your body do you feel tension, and what might it mean?**

My shoulders were tight all day. I realized I'd been holding my breath emotionally. A long exhale in the car reminded me: my body always speaks first.

Day 20

Affirmation: I am awake to the ways I've grown.

How to Implement: **Look back six months—what would the old you be proud of?**

I handled a conflict calmly this week. A few months ago, I would've exploded. That awareness reminded me—I'm not who I was.

Day 21

Affirmation: I see myself clearly and lovingly.

How to Implement: **Write a note to yourself describing your strength.**

I wrote: 'You keep showing up. Even when it's hard. Even when it hurts. That's your strength.' Seeing it in ink made it real.

WEEK 4: March 22–31

Day 22

Affirmation: I give myself permission to feel fully, without apology.

How to Implement: Let yourself cry, laugh, or shout today—without needing a reason.

I cried while washing dishes. Nothing specific triggered it—but I let it happen. That release left me lighter, more human.

Day 23

Affirmation: I no longer numb myself to avoid discomfort.

How to Implement: Notice one distraction you turn to—and try sitting still instead.

I reached for my phone when I felt anxious. This time, I paused. The discomfort was real—but so was my strength to feel it.

Day 24

Affirmation: I allow awareness to guide—not punish—me.

How to Implement: Speak gently to yourself when you notice an old pattern emerge.

I caught myself over-explaining again. Instead of shame, I whispered, 'This is just a habit. I'm learning.' That compassion changed everything.

Day 25

Affirmation: I am safe enough to tell myself the truth.

How to Implement: Write down one truth you've been afraid to face—and sit with it.

I finally wrote, 'I'm not happy here.' That sentence was terrifying. But also, freeing. Awareness isn't the end—it's the beginning.

Day 26

Affirmation: I don't have to understand everything to trust my instincts.

How to Implement: Follow a gut feeling today without overthinking.

I turned down a last-minute invite. Something felt off. Later I heard the energy was chaotic. Trusting myself saved me from burnout.

Day 27

Affirmation: I witness my reactions without shame.

How to Implement: Notice a moment you get triggered—and journal what it taught you.

My heart raced during a conversation. I didn't snap—but I felt the urge. Later, I wrote, 'That reaction is rooted in not being heard.' That's a map to healing.

Day 28

Affirmation: I notice how far I've come—even if others don't.

How to Implement: Celebrate one thing about yourself today—quietly or boldly.

Nobody saw the moment I walked away instead of arguing. But I saw it. And I was proud. That quiet win mattered.

Day 29

Affirmation: I no longer ignore the voice within me.

How to Implement: Ask yourself, 'What do I need right now?'—then listen.

I used to silence my intuition. Now, I pause and ask. One time it said, 'Rest.' And I did. That simple act was revolutionary.

Day 30

Affirmation: I am awake to what I need, not just what I want.

How to Implement: Write a list: needs vs. wants—and prioritize one need today.

I wanted distraction, but I needed peace. So I turned off the noise and sat with myself. That choice made me feel cared for.

Day 31

Affirmation: My awareness is my superpower.

How to Implement: Reflect on three things you've learned about yourself this month.

I learned I still carry anger. I learned I can sit with it. I learned I'm not broken—I'm aware. And that's powerful.

MONTH 4:
ACKNOWLEDGMENT

Name It To Tame It.

This month, we speak our truth without shame. No more pretending. No more minimizing. What happened matters—and so do you.

WEEK 1: April 1–7

Day 1

Affirmation: I honor everything I've survived—without minimizing it.

How to Implement: List one thing you went through that deserves recognition.

I kept brushing off my past like it was no big deal. But the truth is, I've carried heavy things and still moved forward. That deserves more than silence.

Day 2

Affirmation: I speak my truth—even if my voice shakes.

How to Implement: Share a truth with someone you trust—or write it down just for you.

I told my sister I wasn't okay. For once, I didn't sugarcoat it. Her hug was the reward for my honesty.

Day 3

Affirmation: I name my pain so it no longer controls me.

How to Implement: Write one sentence that names what hurt you—without shame.

I wrote: 'He made me feel invisible.' Seeing it in ink helped me take back my power. The pain lost some of its grip.

Day 4

Affirmation: I acknowledge my needs instead of burying them.

How to Implement: **Ask yourself: 'What do I need right now that I haven't said out loud?'**

I kept saying 'I'm just tired,' but the truth was, I needed space. I asked for it—and got it. That felt like self-respect.

Day 5

Affirmation: **I no longer shrink to keep others comfortable.**

How to Implement: **Speak up today in a moment you'd normally stay silent.**

At work, I offered an idea I'd been holding back. No one clapped—but I clapped for myself. That courage mattered.

Day 6

Affirmation: **I can be proud of myself without guilt.**

How to Implement: **Celebrate one personal win today—no matter how small.**

I got out of bed even when depression told me not to. That's a victory. And I don't need applause to call it that.

Day 7

Affirmation: **I acknowledge my progress, not just my flaws.**

How to Implement: **Reflect on one way you've changed for the better this year.**

I used to snap at the smallest things. Now, I pause. That shift didn't happen overnight—but it happened. And I'm proud.

WEEK 2: April 8–14

Day 8

Affirmation: I name my boundaries so others don't cross them.

How to Implement: Say 'no' to something today and watch what happens.

I used to say yes when I meant no. One day, I finally declined an invite without overexplaining. I felt guilty—but also free.

Day 9

Affirmation: I give myself credit for showing up when it was hardest.

How to Implement: Think of a time you kept going—then thank yourself.

No one saw me go to that appointment. But I went, even shaking. I clutched the wheel and whispered, 'You did it.' That moment mattered.

Day 10

Affirmation: I no longer apologize for needing care too.

How to Implement: Ask for support today without shrinking.

I texted my friend, 'Can you just check in on me this week?' It felt weird. But she said, 'Of course.' That moment restored me.

Day 11

Affirmation: I am learning to be seen for who I am—not who I pretend to be.

How to Implement: Share something real with someone safe today.

I told her I wasn't always strong. She didn't flinch. She hugged me. That honesty brought us closer.

Day 12

Affirmation: I can name what I lost—and still be grateful for what remains.

How to Implement: Write down one loss and one lesson it gave you.

I lost a version of myself in that relationship. But I found my voice. That exchange hurt—but gave me back my truth.

Day 13

Affirmation: I honor the wisdom in my scars.

How to Implement: What has one of your wounds taught you? Reflect on it today.

My heartbreak taught me how to set boundaries. My silence taught me how to speak. My pain became my teacher.

Day 14

Affirmation: I'm done pretending I'm fine when I'm not.

How to Implement: Say how you really feel today—even if just to yourself.

Someone asked if I was okay. I said, 'Not really.' No mask, no smile. Just truth. It felt like a breath I hadn't taken in years.

WEEK 3: April 15–21

Day 15

Affirmation: I acknowledge the little girl inside me still waiting to be heard.

How to Implement: Do one kind thing today your younger self would have needed.

I used to push through everything—until I looked at an old photo of myself and whispered, 'You deserved more softness.' That changed the way I show up for myself.

Day 16

Affirmation: I honor my anger as a signal, not a shame.

How to Implement: When anger shows up today, ask: 'What is this trying to protect?'

I snapped at someone and felt guilty. But when I looked closer, I realized I was hurt—not mean. My anger was just a boundary in disguise.

Day 17

Affirmation: I no longer stay silent to keep the peace that breaks me.

How to Implement: Speak your truth in a moment you'd usually stay quiet.

I told him, 'That hurt my feelings.' No yelling, no storm—just truth. The ground didn't shake, but something inside me finally settled.

Day 18

Affirmation: I acknowledge my patterns with curiosity, not criticism.

How to Implement: **Notice one repeated behavior and ask, 'Where did I learn this?'**

I always apologize first—even when I'm not wrong. Turns out, I learned that being quiet kept me safe. Knowing that helped me change it.

Day 19

Affirmation: **I accept compliments without shrinking.**

How to Implement: **When someone praises you today, say 'thank you'—and mean it.**

She told me I was brave. I almost brushed it off. Instead, I breathed in her words like medicine. I believed her.

Day 20

Affirmation: **I acknowledge when something doesn't feel right—and I act on it.**

How to Implement: **Say no to something that doesn't sit well with your spirit.**

I was about to agree to something I didn't want. Then I paused and said, 'Actually, I'm going to pass.' That felt like power.

Day 21

Affirmation: **I give myself permission to be a work in progress.**

How to Implement: **Write down three ways you're healing—even if it's messy.**

I still cry when I remember. I still flinch when I'm surprised. But I also laugh louder now. That's healing, too.

WEEK 4: April 22–30

Day 22

Affirmation: I acknowledge my worth—even when no one else sees it.

How to Implement: Write yourself a short love letter today.

I looked in the mirror and said, 'You matter to me.' No audience, no applause. Just truth between me and my reflection.

Day 23

Affirmation: I no longer gaslight myself into staying small.

How to Implement: Notice when you downplay your feelings—and pause.

I said, 'Maybe it wasn't that bad.' But it was. And I survived. That truth doesn't make me weak—it makes me honest.

Day 24

Affirmation: I allow myself to grow beyond what they expected of me.

How to Implement: Take one bold step today toward the life you want.

They thought I'd stay quiet forever. I didn't. I chose healing, not hiding. That step cracked open a future I hadn't dared imagine.

Day 25

Affirmation: I name my joy as loudly as I name my pain.

How to Implement: Celebrate one thing today—without guilt.

I laughed hard at lunch and caught myself apologizing. Then I stopped. Joy needs no permission.

Day 26

Affirmation: I acknowledge that anger can be sacred—it shows what matters.

How to Implement: Ask: What is my anger trying to protect or restore today?

I was mad because I wasn't being respected. That fire inside wasn't rage—it was clarity.

Day 27

Affirmation: I don't wait for others to validate what I already know.

How to Implement: Say something kind to yourself before anyone else does.

I used to crave praise. Now, I give myself the words I need: 'You're growing. You're doing great.'

Day 28

Affirmation: I accept all parts of me—not just the polished ones.

How to Implement: Write down something imperfect about yourself and bless it.

I overthink everything—but that same mind also helps me notice beauty others miss. That's part of my magic.

Day 29

Affirmation: I acknowledge that healing is nonlinear—and that's okay.

How to Implement: List one way you've grown and one place you're still learning.

I don't cry over the same things anymore. But I still flinch. That doesn't mean I'm broken—it means I'm human.

Day 30

Affirmation: I see myself clearly—and I still choose love.

How to Implement: Look at yourself in silence for one full minute today.

I stood in front of the mirror. No filters, no makeup. Just me. And I said, 'I love you anyway.' That was enough.

MONTH 5:

ACCEPTANCE

It's Not About Giving Up—It's About Letting Go.

This month, we release the grip of control and make peace with what we cannot change. Acceptance is not defeat; it's freedom.

WEEK 1: May 1–7

Day 1

Affirmation: I accept where I am—even as I reach for more.

How to Implement: Name one part of your life you're learning to embrace today.

I used to hate being single. But now I see it as space for me to grow. That shift didn't erase the loneliness—but it gave it purpose.

Day 2

Affirmation: I don't need to be perfect to be worthy of peace.

How to Implement: Write down one 'flaw' you're learning to accept as part of you.

I'm messy when I'm overwhelmed. But that chaos doesn't cancel my kindness. I'm still worthy of love—even when unorganized.

Day 3

Affirmation: I allow things to be both beautiful and broken.

How to Implement: Find something imperfect today—and see the beauty in it.

There's a chipped mug I use every morning. It reminds me that even things with cracks can still be useful, still bring comfort.

Day 4

Affirmation: Acceptance isn't giving up—it's letting go of the fight.

How to Implement: Breathe through one thing you cannot change today.

I kept trying to fix what wasn't mine to fix. One day I whispered, 'I release this.' That didn't make it easier—but it made me lighter.

Day 5

Affirmation: I accept my emotions without labeling them as wrong.

How to Implement: Notice what you're feeling today and just sit with it.

I felt numb today. I didn't try to force joy or clarity—I just let myself feel… nothing. Even that had its own kind of honesty.

Day 6

Affirmation: I am no longer at war with myself.

How to Implement: Say one kind thing to the part of you you usually criticize.

I always hated how sensitive I am. But today, I said, 'That sensitivity helped someone feel seen.' Maybe it's not a weakness after all.

Day 7

Affirmation: I accept the timing of my life—even when it feels off.

How to Implement: Write a note to your future self offering patience.

I thought I'd be further by now. But I reminded myself—growth doesn't follow a calendar. I'm still on time.

WEEK 2: May 8-14

Day 8

Affirmation: I accept the truth of what was—and choose peace over resentment.

How to Implement: Write down one painful truth you've stopped denying.

I used to say, 'It wasn't that bad.' But it was. Accepting that didn't make it okay—it just stopped it from controlling me.

Day 9

Affirmation: I no longer try to edit my story to make others comfortable.

How to Implement: Tell the truth today, even if it's messy.

For years, I left out parts of my story. But the day I said, 'This happened to me'—without apology—I reclaimed my voice.

Day 10

Affirmation: I let go of needing everyone to understand me.

How to Implement: Practice not explaining yourself today.

I said no without a reason. They blinked, confused. I didn't fill the silence—and I didn't feel guilty.

Day 11

Affirmation: I accept my healing process—even when it's not linear.

How to Implement: Note a feeling that's returned and offer it grace.

I thought I was done crying over that situation. Then the tears came again. This time, I didn't shame myself—I just held space.

Day 12

Affirmation: I accept what I can't control and take charge of what I can.

How to Implement: Make a list: what's yours to manage, and what's not.

I realized I was carrying their chaos. I put it down. My peace isn't built on other people changing—it's built on me choosing.

Day 13

Affirmation: I accept that anger is part of my healing—not a flaw.

How to Implement: Let your anger speak to you today—ask it what it needs.

I wasn't just mad. I was hurt. My anger was saying, 'Pay attention.' So I did. And I responded with care, not shame.

Day 14

Affirmation: I allow closure to come from within.

How to Implement: Write the closure letter you never received.

They never apologized. But I wrote, 'You hurt me, and I release you.' I didn't send it—but I felt lighter the moment I finished.

WEEK 3: May 15–21

Day 15

Affirmation: I accept myself in moments of grace and in moments of struggle.

How to Implement: Acknowledge how you're feeling today—without needing to fix it.

I wasn't at my best this morning. I was snappy, tired. But instead of spiraling, I said, 'It's okay to have off days.' That was enough.

Day 16

Affirmation: I no longer force peace—I find it within.

How to Implement: Take five minutes of stillness today and breathe into your body.

I used to fake calm in chaos. Now, I pause, breathe, and find real peace—even if it's quiet and brief.

Day 17

Affirmation: I let go of 'shoulds' and accept what is.

How to Implement: Catch one thought that begins with 'I should'—and reframe it.

I thought, 'I should be over this by now.' Then I said, 'I'm healing at my own pace.' That shift made space for compassion.

Day 18

Affirmation: I am not broken—I'm rebuilding.

How to Implement: **Think of one part of your life you're actively reclaiming.**

After that relationship, I felt ruined. But every time I chose myself, I laid a new brick. I'm not broken—I'm under construction.

Day 19

Affirmation: I accept that forgiveness begins with me.

How to Implement: **Ask: 'What do I need to forgive myself for today?'**

I've held onto guilt like a shield. Today, I said, 'You did your best with what you knew.' That truth gave me peace.

Day 20

Affirmation: I release the need to prove my pain to be believed.

How to Implement: **Let go of explaining yourself to someone who doesn't listen.**

I kept showing receipts to someone who never cared. One day, I deleted the draft. I didn't need their understanding to move on.

Day 21

Affirmation: I accept that love includes boundaries.

How to Implement: **Set a small boundary today with kindness and clarity.**

I said, 'I can't talk about that right now.' It felt awkward—but peaceful. That one sentence honored both me and the relationship.

WEEK 4: May 22–31

Day 22

Affirmation: I accept that not everyone will understand my healing—and that's okay.

How to Implement: Release one person's opinion that's been weighing on you.

I used to need her approval. But today, I chose silence over explanation. That was my freedom.

Day 23

Affirmation: I accept the layers of my story without needing to rewrite them.

How to Implement: Read a journal entry or memory and offer compassion to your past self.

I read an old entry where I blamed myself. I whispered, 'You didn't deserve that.' That moment softened something inside.

Day 24

Affirmation: I let go of who I thought I had to be.

How to Implement: Write a goodbye letter to the version of you that kept pretending.

I wrote: 'You tried so hard to be enough. You can rest now.' That goodbye felt like the start of something new.

Day 25

Affirmation: I accept my voice—even if it trembles.

How to Implement: **Speak your truth in one area where you've held back.**

At dinner, I said, 'Actually, I don't agree.' No yelling—just calm truth. My voice didn't shake—it soared.

Day 26

Affirmation: I embrace stillness without guilt.

How to Implement: **Do nothing for five minutes today—and notice what comes up.**

I sat on the couch and didn't reach for my phone. I just existed. That stillness was strangely healing.

Day 27

Affirmation: I accept that healing is a daily practice, not a destination.

How to Implement: **List three ways you cared for yourself this month.**

I journaled, I cried without shame, and I went outside. Those weren't magic fixes—but they were medicine.

Day 28

Affirmation: I accept love that feels like safety, not survival.

How to Implement: **Reflect on how love has felt—and what you want it to feel like now.**

Love used to mean sacrifice. Now, I want love that breathes with me, not suffocates. I'm allowed to want that.

Day 29

Affirmation: I let go of timelines and honor my pace.

How to Implement: **Choose one area of your life where you'll stop rushing.**

I thought I had to be healed by now. But I'm still waking up and choosing peace. That counts.

Day 30

Affirmation: I accept my softness as strength.

How to Implement: Do something today that lets your tenderness lead.

I comforted a friend and didn't apologize for being emotional. My softness showed up—and made space for theirs.

Day 31

Affirmation: I am enough—even as I continue to grow.

How to Implement: Look at yourself in the mirror and say: 'You are enough.'

I said it three times. I didn't fully believe it at first. But by the third time, something inside me whispered back: 'Yes, you are.'

MONTH 6:
FORGIVENESS

Forgiveness is a gift you give yourself.

This month, we untangle ourselves from the hurt we've carried too long. Not because they deserve it, but because you do.

WEEK 1: June 1–7

Day 1

Affirmation: I forgive myself for what I didn't know then.

How to Implement: Write one lesson your past self was trying to survive through.

I blamed myself for trusting too easily. But back then, I was just craving connection. Now I know better—and that's enough.

Day 2

Affirmation: Forgiveness doesn't mean I condone—it means I choose peace.

How to Implement: Name one thing you're ready to release, even if you'll never forget it.

I kept replaying the hurt. One day, I said, 'This doesn't serve me anymore.' Letting go didn't excuse it—it freed me.

Day 3

Affirmation: I don't have to carry pain to prove it mattered.

How to Implement: Tell yourself: 'My healing doesn't erase my story.'

I thought healing meant forgetting. But every time I choose peace, I honor what I survived.

Day 4

Affirmation: I forgive the version of me who was just trying to cope.

How to Implement: List a behavior you're healing from—and what need it tried to meet.

I used to shut down in conflict. I wasn't cold—I was scared. Naming that helped me soften.

Day 5

Affirmation: I release resentment so it doesn't rot inside me.

How to Implement: Write down what resentment has cost you—then choose something you'd rather carry.

I realized I'd been angry for years. It stole my joy. I'm choosing peace now—not for them, but for me.

Day 6

Affirmation: I forgive—but I still protect myself.

How to Implement: Set a boundary today that honors your healing.

I forgave her, but I don't go back to old dynamics. Forgiveness doesn't mean return—it means release.

Day 7

Affirmation: I forgive myself for the things I did to survive.

How to Implement: Look back with compassion—not judgment.

I said things I regret. But I was in survival mode. Now I say: I see you, I forgive you, and I'm growing from here.

WEEK 2: June 8–14

Day 8

Affirmation: I forgive the silence that left me feeling unseen.

How to Implement: Write about a time you needed someone to speak up for you.

She looked the other way when I needed her most. That silence echoed for years. I no longer let it define my worth.

Day 9

Affirmation: I release the idea that forgiveness means reconnection.

How to Implement: Remind yourself: 'I can forgive and still walk away.'

He apologized. I accepted it. But I didn't invite him back into my life. Forgiveness was a door closing, not reopening.

Day 10

Affirmation: I forgive myself for staying too long—I needed time to see clearly.

How to Implement: Say: 'I gave myself permission to learn at my own pace.'

I kept thinking, 'Why didn't I leave sooner?' But I had to learn the lesson fully. And I did.

Day 11

Affirmation: I release the story that says I was weak for hurting.

How to Implement: Honor one moment when pain made you grow stronger.

That heartbreak shattered me—but it also showed me I could rebuild. That was strength, not weakness.

Day 12

Affirmation: I forgive my past reactions—they were shaped by pain.

How to Implement: Write a letter to the 'you' who lashed out or shut down.

I yelled when I meant to cry. I disappeared when I needed connection. I understand that now—and I forgive her.

Day 13

Affirmation: I choose peace over punishment.

How to Implement: Think of one person you're tired of resenting—and let go of needing revenge.

I kept wishing she'd feel what I felt. But today, I chose peace. That felt like power.

Day 14

Affirmation: I forgive the world for not being fair—and still demand justice.

How to Implement: Name what you deserve—even if you haven't received it yet.

Life hasn't always been kind. But I still believe I'm worthy of love, fairness, and joy. That belief is my protest and my power.

WEEK 3: June 15–21

Day 15

Affirmation: I forgive myself for the times I didn't speak up.

How to Implement: Say aloud: 'I have a right to be heard.'

There were times I bit my tongue just to keep the peace. Now I know—my voice matters too.

Day 16

Affirmation: I let go of anger that no longer protects me.

How to Implement: Ask yourself: What is this anger costing me?

I carried rage like armor. But it started to wear me down. Releasing it made room for rest.

Day 17

Affirmation: I forgive myself for how I survived chaos.

How to Implement: List the survival skills you're ready to release and the ones you want to keep.

I used to check out emotionally. It kept me safe then—but now I want to stay present. That's growth.

Day 18

Affirmation: I accept apologies I never received—for my own healing.

How to Implement: Write: 'I deserved better. I choose healing anyway.'

He never said sorry. But I whispered it to myself and moved forward. That was my closure.

Day 19

Affirmation: I forgive the women I judged before I understood their pain.

How to Implement: Think of one woman you now see differently—send her silent grace.

I used to roll my eyes at her boundaries. Now I realize, she was just protecting her peace. I get it now.

Day 20

Affirmation: I stop punishing myself for trusting the wrong people.

How to Implement: Remind yourself: 'I was open-hearted, not foolish.'

I let the wrong one in. But that doesn't mean I was wrong to love. It means I had hope—and I still do.

Day 21

Affirmation: I forgive myself for the time I wasted on people who weren't ready.

How to Implement: Bless that time as part of your growth—not a loss.

It wasn't wasted—it was preparation. Now I know what I deserve, and I won't settle again.

WEEK 4: June 22–30

Day 22

Affirmation: I forgive myself for needing love in places it couldn't grow.

How to Implement: Say: 'I was worthy, even when they couldn't see it.'

I kept watering dead soil. But now I know—it wasn't me. I was just hoping where hope couldn't live.

Day 23

Affirmation: I release the guilt I was never meant to carry.

How to Implement: Write down one thing that was never your fault.

I thought it was on me to keep everything together. But I was just a kid trying to survive. That guilt was misplaced.

Day 24

Affirmation: I forgive my younger self for not knowing what she knows now.

How to Implement: Look at an old photo of yourself and speak to her gently.

She was doing her best with broken tools. Today, I wrapped her in the words she never heard: 'You are safe now.'

Day 25

Affirmation: I no longer need closure from people who chose confusion.

How to Implement: Let silence be your answer today.

They ghosted me. I waited for explanation. But silence is an answer, and now I respond with distance.

Day 26

Affirmation: I forgive myself for the energy I gave without boundaries.

How to Implement: List one way you'll protect your energy moving forward.

I used to overextend to feel needed. Now, I pause and ask, 'Is this depleting or nourishing?' That changed everything.

Day 27

Affirmation: I accept that healing is sacred—not linear.

How to Implement: Celebrate one small way you showed up for yourself today.

I made the bed. I ate slowly. I didn't apologize for taking up space. That's healing, too.

Day 28

Affirmation: I forgive without forgetting—because I remember to protect myself.

How to Implement: Say: 'I can remember and still release.'

I don't erase the past—I learn from it. Forgiveness means I don't drag it with me.

Day 29

Affirmation: I release the need to replay the worst moments.

How to Implement: When your mind replays pain today, gently say, 'That's over now.'

My thoughts kept circling the betrayal. I whispered, 'We're safe now.' And my body slowly believed me.

Day 30

Affirmation: I forgive myself for how long it took to choose me.

How to Implement: Look in the mirror and say: 'Thank you for coming back.'

I abandoned myself to keep others close. But today, I came home. That return felt like rebirth.

MONTH 7:
UNDERSTANDING

Anger isn't the enemy—confusion is.

This month, we decode our emotional patterns and learn what our anger is really trying to say. Understanding brings clarity.

WEEK 1: July 1–7

Day 1

Affirmation: I seek to understand myself before I seek to be understood.

How to Implement: Take five quiet minutes to check in with how you really feel.

I was angry at everyone. Then I paused and asked, 'What am I actually feeling?' Turned out, it was grief wearing armor.

Day 2

Affirmation: Understanding my story helps me write a new one.

How to Implement: Journal about one moment that shaped how you view yourself.

That breakup wrecked me—but it also showed me how much I'd been settling. Understanding that shifted my whole standard.

Day 3

Affirmation: I am not my reactions—I am my awareness of them.

How to Implement: Notice one reaction today and ask yourself what triggered it.

I snapped at my sister. Later I realized—I felt unseen. That insight softened everything.

Day 4

Affirmation: I offer myself grace when I don't get it right.

How to Implement: Say: 'I am learning. I am not failing.'

I missed a boundary again. But instead of spiraling, I said, 'I noticed. That's growth.'

Day 5

Affirmation: I listen to understand, not just to respond.

How to Implement: In your next conversation, focus on really hearing—not fixing.

She didn't want advice. She just wanted presence. That understanding made me a better sister.

Day 6

Affirmation: I understand that anger is often unspoken need.

How to Implement: Ask your anger: 'What are you trying to protect?'

My outburst wasn't just rage—it was fear. Once I named it, I could soothe it instead of judging it.

Day 7

Affirmation: Understanding leads to compassion—not excuses.

How to Implement: Think of someone who hurt you. Say: 'I understand, but I still choose me.'

I saw why he acted that way. But understanding him didn't mean I stayed. It meant I left with peace.

WEEK 2: July 8–14

Day 8

Affirmation: I honor the root before I judge the fruit.

How to Implement: Trace a current behavior back to its emotional root.

I avoid closeness. At first I blamed myself. Then I realized—I was taught distance was safety.

Day 9

Affirmation: I make space for complexity—I don't need to be one thing.

How to Implement: List three things you are, even if they seem contradictory.

I can be healing and still hurting. Strong and soft. Angry and loving. I am not a contradiction—I'm layered.

Day 10

Affirmation: I understand my triggers so I can tend to my wounds.

How to Implement: Notice what triggered you today and offer yourself care—not shame.

When she raised her voice, I flinched. It reminded me of old fights. That awareness helped me breathe instead of react.

Day 11

Affirmation: I release the need to be understood by everyone.

How to Implement: Affirm: 'I don't owe understanding to people committed to misunderstanding me.'

Some folks just want to argue. When I stopped explaining, I found peace they couldn't disrupt.

Day 12

Affirmation: Understanding myself helps me choose healthier love.

How to Implement: Write what you now need from love that you didn't ask for before.

I used to think love meant self-sacrifice. Now I ask for presence, peace, and patience.

Day 13

Affirmation: I offer understanding without abandoning my boundaries.

How to Implement: Hold space for someone today without shrinking yourself.

She vented for an hour. I listened—but still said, 'I need to rest now.' That balance felt like power.

Day 14

Affirmation: I seek understanding, not control.

How to Implement: Let go of needing to 'fix' someone else's choices today.

I wanted to make her see things my way. But I paused. I chose understanding over control—and peace followed.

WEEK 3: July 15–21

Day 15

Affirmation: I understand my patterns so I can rewrite them.

How to Implement: Reflect on one pattern you're actively changing.

I kept choosing people who didn't choose me. Then I realized—I was reenacting abandonment. Awareness changed everything.

Day 16

Affirmation: I give myself the patience I once begged for.

How to Implement: Pause when you're frustrated with yourself and say: 'You're allowed to take time.'

I used to rush my healing. Now I say, 'We're not late—we're learning.' That patience is my peace.

Day 17

Affirmation: I don't need to justify my healing to anyone.

How to Implement: Affirm: 'This journey is mine—and I honor it.'

She asked, 'Why are you still in therapy?' I smiled and said, 'Because I matter.' That was enough.

Day 18

Affirmation: I understand that growth often feels like grief.

How to Implement: Write about something you had to leave behind in order to grow.

I let go of a friend I loved. Not because she was bad—but because I wasn't the same. That grief was sacred.

Day 19

Affirmation: I listen inward more than I look outward.

How to Implement: Spend five minutes listening to your inner voice—not your critics.

I checked in with me—not the group chat. What I needed was already within.

Day 20

Affirmation: I extend understanding to myself in moments of doubt.

How to Implement: When self-doubt creeps in, respond with truth—not judgment.

I doubted if I was strong enough. Then I looked back at all I'd overcome. That reminder was louder than my fear.

Day 21

Affirmation: Understanding my needs helps me communicate with love.

How to Implement: State a need today with clarity and kindness.

I said, 'I need some alone time to reset.' It wasn't rude—it was respectful. Understanding myself helped me express it well.

WEEK 4: July 22–31

Day 22

Affirmation: I understand that my peace is not selfish.

How to Implement: Say: 'Choosing peace is choosing me.'

I used to feel guilty resting. Now I know—my peace is my protest.

Day 23

Affirmation: I let go of needing to explain myself to be valid.

How to Implement: **Affirm: 'I am clear within. That's enough.'**

I stopped justifying why I left. I knew. That clarity became my closure.

Day 24

Affirmation: I understand that boundaries build bridges to real connection.

How to Implement: **Set one boundary today with firmness and love.**

I said, 'Please don't raise your voice at me.' It wasn't a wall—it was a door to better communication.

Day 25

Affirmation: I listen to my triggers without letting them take the wheel.

How to Implement: **When triggered today, pause and ask: 'What needs my attention?'**

The tone reminded me of old wounds. Instead of reacting, I checked in with myself. That pause protected me.

Day 26

Affirmation: I give myself permission to outgrow what no longer fits.

How to Implement: Name one role or relationship you've outgrown and why.

I was the fixer for too long. But healing showed me: I'm not here to save—I'm here to be whole.

Day 27

Affirmation: I understand that anger often masks hurt.

How to Implement: Ask: 'What's beneath my anger today?'

I was snapping all day. Then I realized—I felt invisible. Understanding that softened my edge.

Day 28

Affirmation: I choose understanding over assumptions.

How to Implement: Before assuming, ask a clarifying question today.

Instead of stewing, I said, 'Hey, what did you mean by that?' The truth surprised me—in a good way.

Day 29

Affirmation: I understand that not all storms are meant to be weathered.

How to Implement: Walk away from one thing today that's costing you peace.

I used to stay and try harder. Now I walk away when peace isn't present. That's growth.

Day 30

Affirmation: I give grace to my process.

How to Implement: Write: 'I am allowed to take the long way.'

Some days I sprint. Some days I crawl. Both are progress.

Day 31

Affirmation: I understand myself more deeply every day—and that's a gift.

How to Implement: Reflect on how far you've come in your self-awareness.

Five years ago, I wouldn't have known what I needed. Today, I name it, claim it, and choose it.

MONTH 8:

FAITH

You don't have to see the whole path to take the first step.

This month, we trust the process, even when it feels uncertain. Your healing is already in motion.

WEEK 1: August 1–7

Day 1

Affirmation: I trust that what's meant for me won't miss me.

How to Implement: Say: 'If it passed me, it wasn't mine to carry.'

He chose someone else. That used to crush me. Now I say, 'That wasn't my blessing—it was my lesson.'

Day 2

Affirmation: I have faith in my ability to begin again.

How to Implement: Reflect on a time you thought it was over—but found a new way.

I thought the divorce was the end. But it became the beginning of my freedom.

Day 3

Affirmation: I trust the timing of my healing.

How to Implement: Affirm: 'I am not behind—I am on time for my own life.'

Others moved on faster. I'm still rebuilding. And that's okay. Faith lets me grow at my pace.

Day 4

Affirmation: I believe in my resilience—even when I feel fragile.

How to Implement: List three ways you've kept going when it was hard.

I kept showing up. I kept breathing. I kept trying. That's resilience, even when it didn't feel like it.

Day 5

Affirmation: I have faith that my softness is not weakness.

How to Implement: Do something kind for yourself today without justification.

I used to equate toughness with strength. Now I know—gentleness can be a radical act of power.

Day 6

Affirmation: I trust that I can create new stories from old pain.

How to Implement: Write a new narrative for an old wound.

He hurt me. But I didn't stay bitter—I became better. That rewrite saved me.

Day 7

Affirmation: I believe there's more ahead of me than behind me.

How to Implement: Say out loud: 'The best parts of my story haven't even happened yet.'

I looked at my past like a closed door. Now I see it as the foundation. What's ahead is still unwritten—and I'm the author.

WEEK 2: August 8–14

Day 8

Affirmation: I trust the process, even when it's unclear.

How to Implement: Say: 'I don't need all the answers to keep moving forward.'

I was used to needing control. But when I leaned into faith, the next step always found me.

Day 9

Affirmation: I believe that my healing is unfolding in divine order.

How to Implement: **Affirm: 'Even delays carry purpose.'**

When the job fell through, I felt lost. But that pause gave me space to rediscover what I truly wanted.

Day 10

Affirmation: I trust that rest is a part of growth.

How to Implement: **Take a moment to rest without guilt today.**

I used to think hustle meant progress. But I grew more when I paused and listened inward.

Day 11

Affirmation: I have faith that life will meet me where I'm ready.

How to Implement: **List one way you've grown that prepared you for what's next.**

Back then, I wasn't ready for healthy love. Now I am—and I trust it's on the way.

Day 12

Affirmation: I believe in what I cannot yet see.

How to Implement: Say: 'Just because it's not visible doesn't mean it's not real.'

Like a seed underground, I trust that my work is growing something—even in silence.

Day 13

Affirmation: I trust that my intuition is a sacred guide.

How to Implement: Listen to one gut instinct today—and honor it.

I ignored my intuition for years. But the moment I listened, I felt safe again.

Day 14

Affirmation: I believe that surrender is strength, not weakness.

How to Implement: Release one thing you've been tightly gripping—mentally or emotionally.

I tried to control the outcome. But surrendering brought peace, not loss. That surprised me—and healed me.

WEEK 3: August 15–21

Day 15

Affirmation: I trust that what I release creates space for what I need.

How to Implement: Let go of one thought, item, or emotion that's weighing you down.

I held onto old texts like they held answers. Today, I deleted them—and felt lighter.

Day 16

Affirmation: I believe that peace is a possibility for me.

How to Implement: Visualize yourself in peace—even if it feels far away.

For years, chaos felt normal. Now, when it's quiet, I don't fear it—I breathe it in.

Day 17

Affirmation: I trust that love begins with how I treat myself.

How to Implement: Do one loving thing for yourself today without apology.

I took myself out, smiled in the mirror, and said, 'You're worth showing up for.' That changed my whole day.

Day 18

Affirmation: I believe that nothing is wasted—not even my pain.

How to Implement: Name one lesson you learned through a hard experience.

The betrayal hurt deeply. But it taught me how to trust my instincts—and that's priceless.

Day 19

Affirmation: I have faith that I'm becoming the woman I once needed.

How to Implement: Write: 'I am proud of who I'm becoming.'

The girl I was didn't know peace. But the woman I am creates it daily. That's faith in action.

Day 20

Affirmation: I trust that I'm aligned with something greater than fear.

How to Implement: Say: 'Fear is not my final answer.'

I used to let fear make decisions. Now I ask, 'What would faith choose?' Then I follow that.

Day 21

Affirmation: I believe that rest, joy, and love are not rewards—I'm already worthy of them.

How to Implement: Give yourself one moment of joy today—on purpose.

I laughed without guilt. I rested without earning it. I let love in without needing to prove myself.

WEEK 4: August 22–31

Day 22

Affirmation: I trust that every closed door is divine redirection.

How to Implement: Reflect on one 'no' that protected you.

I wanted that relationship to work. Now I thank God it didn't. It saved me from settling.

Day 23

Affirmation: I believe that peace is my birthright, not a prize.

How to Implement: Say: 'I don't have to earn peace—I can choose it now.'

Peace used to feel distant. Now, I create it in small ways—deep breaths, gentle thoughts, soft mornings.

Day 24

Affirmation: I trust my journey, even when others don't understand it.

How to Implement: Affirm: 'I don't need permission to heal.'

They didn't get why I moved on. But I did it anyway—and it made room for everything I prayed for.

Day 25

Affirmation: I believe I am supported, even when I feel alone.

How to Implement: List the unseen ways you are held—by ancestors, by spirit, by self.

I felt abandoned. But then I remembered who prayed for me before I even arrived. That's support I carry daily.

Day 26

Affirmation: I have faith that I'll rise again—no matter how many times I fall.

How to Implement: Write about a moment you got back up.

After the breakdown, I made breakfast. That small act was a resurrection.

Day 27

Affirmation: I trust my future because I'm healing my present.

How to Implement: Say: 'The work I do now creates the peace I want later.'

Every time I set a boundary, rest, or forgive myself—I'm building a future I can breathe in.

Day 28

Affirmation: I believe in joy as part of healing—not just the reward at the end.

How to Implement: Do something joyful today, even if it's small.

I danced while folding laundry. It wasn't much—but it reminded me joy doesn't wait.

Day 29

Affirmation: I trust that clarity comes when I'm still enough to receive it.

How to Implement: Practice stillness today for at least five minutes.

I used to chase answers. Now I sit, breathe, and let clarity find me.

Day 30

Affirmation: I have faith that who I'm becoming is already within me.

How to Implement: Look in the mirror and say: 'She's already here.'

I used to hope to become her. Now I know—I've been her all along. Faith helped me see it.

Day 31

Affirmation: I believe that my story matters—and it's still unfolding.

How to Implement: Say: 'My voice has value. My story holds power.'

Even in the messy chapters, I speak. Because healing doesn't mean silence—it means wholeness.

MONTH 9:

TRUST

You deserve to feel safe—even with yourself.

This month, we rebuild trust with our own voice, our intuition, and the people who prove they're safe. One boundary at a time.

R4WEEK 1: September 1–7

Day 1

Affirmation: I trust myself to make decisions that honor my peace.

How to Implement: Before acting today, pause and ask: 'Does this protect my peace?'

I used to second-guess everything. But when I chose peace as my compass, clarity followed.

Day 2

Affirmation: I trust that I am not too much—I am just enough for the right spaces.

How to Implement: **Affirm:** 'I do not shrink for comfort—I stand in my fullness.'

When I stopped apologizing for being loud, passionate, emotional—I found people who loved me for all of it.

Day 3

Affirmation: I trust that what I feel is valid—even if others don't understand it.

How to Implement: Give your emotions space today without explaining them away.

I cried without rushing to say, 'I'm fine.' That truth felt like freedom.

Day 4

Affirmation: I trust that my boundaries protect what I've worked hard to build.

How to Implement: Say no today, even if it feels uncomfortable.

Every time I say 'no,' I say 'yes' to myself. That's trust in action.

Day 5

Affirmation: I trust the wisdom of my body when it asks me to slow down.

How to Implement: Rest when you need to. Your worth isn't in your productivity.

I pushed myself for years. Now, when my body whispers 'rest,' I listen.

Day 6

Affirmation: I trust myself to walk away from what no longer aligns.

How to Implement: Think about one thing you've outgrown—and bless your release of it.

The old version of me needed that chaos. The healed version chooses quiet instead.

Day 7

Affirmation: I trust the timing of my life—even the parts that feel delayed.

How to Implement: Write: 'This moment is not punishment. It's preparation.'

I thought I was falling behind. Turns out, I was being positioned for something greater.

WEEK 2: September 8–14

Day 8

Affirmation: I trust that my story has power—even the parts I used to hide.

How to Implement: Speak your truth today, even if only to yourself.

I kept quiet for years. But when I finally spoke my pain, it stopped owning me.

Day 9

Affirmation: I trust my voice—it knows what I need.

How to Implement: Say what you need out loud today—even if no one else hears it.

I whispered, 'I want more.' That quiet confession was the start of my transformation.

Day 10

Affirmation: I trust that letting go doesn't mean I failed—it means I'm free.

How to Implement: Release something today you've been gripping in fear.

I let go of the need to be understood—and gained peace instead.

Day 11

Affirmation: I trust the woman I'm becoming.

How to Implement: **Look at an old picture of yourself. Honor how far you've come.**

She had no idea she'd survive all that. I honor her by trusting who I am now.

Day 12

Affirmation: I trust that vulnerability is strength, not weakness.

How to Implement: **Share one real feeling today with someone safe—or with your journal.**

I said, 'I'm not okay today.' That softness brought connection, not shame.

Day 13

Affirmation: I trust that setbacks don't erase my progress.

How to Implement: **Remind yourself: 'A slip is not a spiral.'**

I had a rough day—but I didn't stay there. Trust kept me grounded.

Day 14

Affirmation: I trust that what I give myself, I teach others to give me too.

How to Implement: **Practice self-respect today—and notice how others follow.**

When I spoke to myself kindly, others did too. That trust reshaped my relationships.

WEEK 3: September 15–21

Day 15

Affirmation: I trust that I am worthy of love that doesn't hurt.

How to Implement: Affirm: 'I don't have to earn what I deserve.'

I used to mistake chaos for passion. Now, I only call it love if it feels like peace.

Day 16

Affirmation: I trust that saying no is an act of self-trust.

How to Implement: Say no today without guilt or over-explaining.

I used to say yes to avoid tension. But every no I say now reinforces my freedom.

Day 17

Affirmation: I trust my instincts—even when they go against the crowd.

How to Implement: Follow your gut today on one decision—big or small.

They all said stay. My gut said go. I listened—and never regretted it.

Day 18

Affirmation: I trust that the life I'm building doesn't need to look like anyone else's.

How to Implement: List three things about your journey that are uniquely yours.

I don't follow templates anymore. I follow truth—and that's enough.

Day 19

Affirmation: I trust the pauses as much as the progress.

How to Implement: Give yourself grace if today is slower than expected.

Some days I only rest. That's not laziness—it's listening.

Day 20

Affirmation: I trust that old survival habits no longer serve my healed self.

How to Implement: Notice one habit rooted in fear that you're ready to release.

I always over-explained. Now I just state it once—with calm and confidence.

Day 21

Affirmation: I trust that peace won't require me to betray myself.

How to Implement: Stay true to yourself in at least one interaction today.

I used to agree just to keep the peace. Now I understand—if I lose myself, it's not real peace.

WEEK 4: September 22–30

Day 22

Affirmation: I trust that my boundaries are acts of love—not rejection.

How to Implement: Set one clear boundary today without apology.

I used to feel bad saying no. Now I know—my boundaries teach people how to love me right.

Day 23

Affirmation: I trust that I can be soft and still be safe.

How to Implement: Give yourself permission to soften in one area today.

I learned to armor up to survive. Now, I allow softness—and realize I'm still protected.

Day 24

Affirmation: I trust that distance can be a form of self-respect.

How to Implement: Take space where it's needed without guilt.

I didn't ghost them. I honored my energy. That's the difference.

Day 25

Affirmation: I trust the truth—even when it hurts.

How to Implement: Name one truth you're ready to face without flinching.

It wasn't love—it was attachment. Facing that truth set me free.

Day 26

Affirmation: I trust that joy doesn't require struggle as a prerequisite.

How to Implement: Let yourself experience joy today without justification.

For once, I didn't brace for the other shoe. I let myself laugh—and that was enough.

Day 27

Affirmation: I trust that clarity grows in silence.

How to Implement: Spend five minutes today in quiet reflection.

I stopped chasing signs and sat in silence. That's when the knowing came.

Day 28

Affirmation: I trust that forgiveness sets *me* free.

How to Implement: Forgive one small thing today—not for them, for you.

I forgave someone who never apologized. Not because they deserved it, but because I did.

Day 29

Affirmation: I trust that anger can be a teacher—not just a reaction.

How to Implement: Ask: 'What is my anger trying to show me today?'

My anger said, 'You keep tolerating what hurts you.' That truth became my compass.

Day 30

Affirmation: I trust that healing is worth the effort—even on hard days.

How to Implement: Remind yourself: 'I didn't come this far to abandon myself now.'

Healing isn't linear—but every step I take honors the version of me that once felt broken.

MONTH 10:

WORTH

You don't have to earn your value.

This month, we unlearn the lie that we are only as good as we produce, perform, or please. You are already enough.

WEEK 1: October 1–7

Day 1

Affirmation: I am worthy—without performance, perfection, or permission.

How to Implement: Say: 'I don't have to prove my worth. I already have it.'

I used to chase validation. Now I sit in my value, knowing nothing outside me defines it.

Day 2

Affirmation: I am not what I produce. I am who I am—and that's enough.

How to Implement: Rest today without trying to earn it.

When I stopped overworking for approval, I discovered rest as resistance—and reclamation.

Day 3

Affirmation: I am worthy of softness—even when I've been hardened by life.

How to Implement: Do one gentle thing for yourself today.

The world toughened me up, but healing taught me I deserve tenderness, too.

Day 4

Affirmation: I don't have to earn love—I only have to receive it.

How to Implement: Affirm: 'I am lovable as I am.'

I broke the habit of chasing those who couldn't love me. Now I wait for love that sees me clearly.

Day 5

Affirmation: I am worthy of being seen in my wholeness—not just in my struggle.

How to Implement: Let yourself be celebrated today, not just tolerated.

I used to be valued for how much I could carry. Now I am loved for simply being me.

Day 6

Affirmation: I am not too much. I am exactly enough.

How to Implement: Say: 'I will not shrink to be digestible.'

Every time I muted myself to be accepted, I betrayed myself. I don't do that anymore.

Day 7

Affirmation: I am worthy of new beginnings—no matter how messy the past.

How to Implement: Write: 'I get to start over, as many times as I need.'

Starting again doesn't mean I failed. It means I'm still choosing myself.

WEEK 2: October 8–14

Day 8

Affirmation: I am worthy of boundaries that protect my peace.

How to Implement: Enforce one boundary today—even if it's uncomfortable.

They rolled their eyes when I said no. I didn't budge. That was my healing in action.

Day 9

Affirmation: I am worthy of joy without guilt.

How to Implement: Give yourself a joyful moment and soak it in fully.

I laughed hard today—and didn't question if I deserved it. That freedom was sacred.

Day 10

Affirmation: I am worthy of taking up space—physically, emotionally, spiritually.

How to Implement: Take up space today without shrinking—speak, move, breathe fully.

I stopped making myself small to avoid making others uncomfortable.

Day 11

Affirmation: I am worthy of releasing what no longer reflects my growth.

How to Implement: Let go of one object, thought, or connection that no longer fits you.

I donated the clothes I wore when I tolerated less. I'm dressing for my worth now.

Day 12

Affirmation: I am worthy of rest that restores, not just rest that recovers.

How to Implement: Plan one moment of rest that's just for joy—not exhaustion.

I used to rest only when I collapsed. Now I rest because I deserve softness every day.

Day 13

Affirmation: I am worthy of speaking up—my voice matters.

How to Implement: Say what you need today, even if it shakes your voice.

I was silent for years. Today, I said, 'This hurts.' And that truth changed the room.

Day 14

Affirmation: I am worthy of forgiveness—especially from myself.

How to Implement: Write: 'I forgive myself for…' and finish the sentence.

I blamed myself for staying too long. Now I thank myself for leaving when I did.

WEEK 3: October 15–21

Day 15

Affirmation: I am worthy of love that feels safe, steady, and soul-deep.

How to Implement: Reflect on how you want love to feel—not just look.

I used to settle for excitement. Now I crave calm love—the kind that doesn't confuse peace with boredom.

Day 16

Affirmation: I am worthy of letting go of survival mode.

How to Implement: Take one deep breath and tell your body: 'We're safe now.'

I always braced for impact. Today, I told myself, 'You can exhale now.'

Day 17

Affirmation: I am worthy of evolving beyond who others think I should be.

How to Implement: Do one thing today that aligns with who you are now—not who you were.

They expect the old me. I show up as the healed me anyway.

Day 18

Affirmation: I am worthy of experiences that nourish my spirit.

How to Implement: Say yes to something that feels soul-satisfying—even if it's small.

I took a walk alone and watched the sky shift. That stillness filled me in a way applause never could.

Day 19

Affirmation: I am worthy of not rushing my healing.

How to Implement: Give yourself permission to take your time today.

I tried to fast-track healing like a checklist. Now I treat it like a garden—tended, not timed.

Day 20

Affirmation: I am worthy of softness even when I make mistakes.

How to Implement: Respond to yourself with kindness after a slip today.

I snapped. I apologized. But I didn't spiral. I gave myself grace—and kept going.

Day 21

Affirmation: I am worthy of building a life that reflects my healing—not my hurt.

How to Implement: Look around and ask: 'Does this reflect the healed me?'

I changed my environment to match my growth. My peace started with where I woke up.

WEEK 4: October 22–31

Day 22

Affirmation: I am worthy of keeping promises to myself.

How to Implement: Follow through on one commitment you made to yourself today.

I always showed up for others. Showing up for me? That's a new kind of love.

Day 23

Affirmation: I am worthy of being loved in my wholeness—not just my healing.

How to Implement: Remind yourself: 'I don't have to be fixed to be loved.'

They loved the comeback story. I wanted someone who loved the whole book.

Day 24

Affirmation: I am worthy of relationships where I feel safe—not just needed.

How to Implement: Notice who honors your feelings—not just your labor.

I'm no longer building homes in people who only call when they're broken.

Day 25

Affirmation: I am worthy of joy that isn't interrupted by shame.

How to Implement: Say yes to something fun—and don't explain it away.

I danced alone in the kitchen and smiled. That joy was mine to keep.

Day 26

Affirmation: I am worthy of peace that lasts longer than a moment.

How to Implement: Create one peaceful ritual you can return to anytime.

I light a candle and breathe. It's simple—but now, peace feels accessible.

Day 27

Affirmation: I am worthy of evolving—even when it makes others uncomfortable.

How to Implement: Don't apologize for your growth today.

She said, 'You've changed.' I said, 'Thank you.'

Day 28

Affirmation: I am worthy of being chosen—by others, and by myself.

How to Implement: Choose yourself today in one big or small way.

For once, I didn't wait to be picked. I picked me.

Day 29

Affirmation: I am worthy of keeping the softness I fought to reclaim.

How to Implement: Protect your softness like it's sacred—because it is.

They tried to harden me. I chose healing instead.

Day 30

Affirmation: I am worthy of my own compassion—especially on hard days.

How to Implement: Give yourself the grace you often extend to others.

Today I cried and didn't rush to fix it. I just held myself through it.

Day 31

Affirmation: I am worthy of writing a new story, starting now.

How to Implement: Write: 'The next chapter of my life will feel like ___.'

I'm not who I was when I started. And that's the story I'm proud to tell.

MONTH 11:
SERVICE

Give from your overflow, not your exhaustion.

This month, we redefine what it means to serve—with joy, clarity, and boundaries. Your purpose deserves your protection.

WEEK 1: November 1–7

Day 1

Affirmation: I serve best when I include myself in the care I give.

How to Implement: Do one act of service for yourself today.

I used to pour from an empty cup. Now, I fill mine first—and what overflows is my gift.

Day 2

Affirmation: I don't have to abandon myself to support others.

How to Implement: Set a limit today that allows you to give without resentment.

I thought saying yes meant I was kind. But real kindness doesn't come with bitterness.

Day 3

Affirmation: I can be of service without being a savior.

How to Implement: Offer help without taking on someone else's healing journey.

I used to carry other people's pain like it was mine. Now I walk beside, not in place of.

Day 4

Affirmation: Service that costs my peace is too expensive.

How to Implement: Pause and ask: 'Is this aligned with love or obligation?'

I said yes out of guilt. It drained me. Now I serve from clarity, not compulsion.

Day 5

Affirmation: I am allowed to rest even when others keep going.

How to Implement: Rest today as an act of resistance and self-respect.

The world kept spinning. I stopped. And nothing fell apart.

Day 6

Affirmation: My presence is service—not just my doing.

How to Implement: Be fully present in one interaction today without fixing or performing.

I listened without offering advice. That moment of presence was the most powerful gift.

Day 7

Affirmation: I serve more powerfully when I'm aligned, not exhausted.

How to Implement: Do something today that re-centers you before giving to others.

I lit incense, breathed deep, and found myself again. Then I gave—from overflow, not depletion.

WEEK 2: November 8–14

Day 8

Affirmation: I serve my purpose best when I am aligned with my truth.

How to Implement: Do one thing today that feels deeply aligned with your values.

I stopped chasing what looked good and followed what felt true. That's when my service deepened.

Day 9

Affirmation: I do not need to overextend to prove I'm enough.

How to Implement: Give only what you can give freely, without depletion.

I used to say yes to feel worthy. Now I say yes because it feels right.

Day 10

Affirmation: Service rooted in love transforms—not controls.

How to Implement: Help someone today without expectation or attachment to the outcome.

I let go of trying to fix others. I hold space now—that's enough.

Day 11

Affirmation: I am not responsible for everyone's happiness.

How to Implement: Release the pressure to make others okay today.

Their peace is not mine to manufacture. I can offer kindness without carrying their burdens.

Day 12

Affirmation: Service includes uplifting voices besides my own.

How to Implement: Amplify someone else's truth today.

I used to need the spotlight to feel seen. Now I share it—and feel more powerful.

Day 13

Affirmation: I am worthy of serving from joy—not martyrdom.

How to Implement: Do something today that brings joy to both you and the one you serve.

When I served with joy, not sacrifice, I found energy I didn't know I had.

Day 14

Affirmation: I serve most powerfully when I'm honest about my capacity.

How to Implement: Tell the truth if you're not available today. That's integrity, not failure.

I said, 'I can't today.' And they understood. Turns out I wasn't the only one tired.

WEEK 3: November 15–21

Day 15

Affirmation: I can serve others without sacrificing myself.

How to Implement: Say no to one request today that would drain you unnecessarily.

I used to believe love meant self-sacrifice. I showed up even when I was breaking inside. Then one day, I said no—to them, but yes to me. It was terrifying. But that 'no' became the first brick in rebuilding my peace.

Day 16

Affirmation: My compassion includes myself.

How to Implement: Practice self-kindness in how you speak to yourself today.

I gave grace to everyone but me. When I finally told myself, 'You're doing your best,' I cried. That one sentence felt like a hug I'd needed for years.

Day 17

Affirmation: I can serve with love, not codependency.

How to Implement: Offer support without trying to fix someone else's problem today.

She called me, spiraling again. I listened, but I didn't fix it this time. I said, 'I trust you'll figure this out.' I hung up knowing I helped without abandoning myself.

Day 18

Affirmation: Serving from overflow is sustainable—serving from emptiness is not.

How to Implement: Take 10 minutes today to restore your energy before offering it to others.

I was the 'strong one.' Everyone leaned on me, and I let them. But strength with no rest turned me bitter. When I started putting myself first, I found joy again in being of service.

Day 19

Affirmation: I don't have to do everything to make a difference.

How to Implement: Pick one intentional act of kindness today, not ten.

I baked cookies for one friend instead of volunteering at three events. She said it made her whole week. Sometimes small is sacred.

Day 20

Affirmation: I am not my usefulness. I am worthy without proving it.

How to Implement: Affirm: 'I don't have to earn my place through labor.'

The day I sat in a room and didn't offer to help, didn't clean, didn't fix—I just existed—I realized I was still loved. Still welcome. Still enough.

Day 21

Affirmation: I can serve others without abandoning my joy.

How to Implement: Do something today that brings you joy first, before helping anyone else.

I used to dim my light so others could shine. But one day, I sang before I served, danced before I gave. That joy made my offering richer.

WEEK 4: November 22–30

Day 22

Affirmation: I am allowed to rest—even when the world is still spinning.

How to Implement: Give yourself permission to do nothing for a while today.

I used to feel guilty for resting, like the world would fall apart if I paused. One day I took a nap instead of running one more errand—and nothing collapsed. Except the belief that I had to earn rest.

Day 23

Affirmation: I honor myself by honoring my limits.

How to Implement: Say, 'That's enough for today,' and let it be true.

Burnout was my badge of honor for too long. But now, stopping at enough is my act of strength.

Day 24

Affirmation: I can say no without explaining, defending, or feeling guilty.

How to Implement: Practice a clean, unapologetic 'no' today.

When I stopped over-explaining every no, I realized I didn't owe anyone a performance—just my truth.

Day 25

Affirmation: Service is sacred when it's chosen—not coerced.

How to Implement: Say yes today only if it comes from peace, not pressure.

I used to say yes out of fear of being disliked. Now I only say yes if my soul agrees.

Day 26

Affirmation: I can serve without being the strong one all the time.

How to Implement: Let someone support *you* today—even in a small way.

I was the rock for everyone. Until I cracked. Asking for help didn't make me weak—it made me real.

Day 27

Affirmation: My softness is not a weakness—it's my superpower.

How to Implement: Lead with gentleness in one conversation today.

I thought I had to be hard to survive. But when I softened, people leaned in—not away.

Day 28

Affirmation: I am more than what I give—I am someone worth receiving.

How to Implement: Receive something today without offering anything in return.

I used to deflect compliments, gifts, love. Then one day, I just said, 'Thank you.' That moment changed everything.

Day 29

Affirmation: **Saying less is sometimes the most generous gift I can give.**

How to Implement: **Pause before speaking today, and offer your presence instead.**

I used to fill silence to soothe others' discomfort. But my quiet sometimes said more than words ever could.

Day 30

Affirmation: **I serve through being, not just doing.**

How to Implement: **Sit still today and let your energy be your offering.**

The more I became at peace with myself, the more peace I brought into the room—without lifting a finger.

MONTH 12:
PEACE

Peace isn't passive—it's a choice.

This month, we choose softness over struggle, clarity over chaos, and truth over silence. You've earned your calm.

WEEK 1: December 1–7

Day 1

Affirmation: **Peace is not a destination—it's a practice.**

How to Implement: **Start your morning with five minutes of stillness.**

I thought peace was somewhere I had to arrive. Then I realized it was in the pause between breaths—always available, if I chose it.

Day 2

Affirmation: **I do not chase peace—I choose it.**

How to Implement: **Decline one thing today that disturbs your calm.**

I used to rearrange my life for approval. Now I rearrange it for peace—and that shift changed everything.

Day 3

Affirmation: **Peace grows when I release what I can't control.**

How to Implement: **Write down what's out of your hands—and let it go.**

I gripped the steering wheel of life so tight my knuckles hurt. The day I unclenched, I found space to breathe.

Day 4

Affirmation: **I protect my peace like I protect my healing—it's sacred.**

How to Implement: **Reinforce one boundary today to guard your inner calm.**

Peace wasn't a bubble bath. It was saying 'no' without guilt and 'yes' without fear.

Day 5

Affirmation: My peace matters more than being understood.

How to Implement: Let go of needing to explain your healing to others.

They didn't get it, and that used to bother me. Now I realize—my peace doesn't need an audience.

Day 6

Affirmation: Peace begins where self-judgment ends.

How to Implement: Replace one harsh thought today with kindness.

I caught myself calling me 'lazy' for resting. Then I said, 'You're recovering.' That reframing gave me grace.

Day 7

Affirmation: I do not earn peace—I return to it.

How to Implement: Take a walk, sit in nature, or breathe—just return to your calm center.

Every time I got overwhelmed, I thought I failed. But peace isn't lost—it's just waiting for me to return.

WEEK 2: December 8–14

Day 8

Affirmation: My peace doesn't depend on others' behavior.

How to Implement: Notice how you respond when someone else is upset—choose not to absorb it.

Their chaos used to become mine. Now I leave their storm at their doorstep and return to my calm.

Day 9

Affirmation: Silence can be healing, not punishment.

How to Implement: Take a quiet moment today without explanation.

I used to fear silence—it felt like rejection. Now, it feels like a warm bath for my nervous system.

Day 10

Affirmation: I honor my nervous system by slowing down.

How to Implement: Say no to rushing today. Let things unfold slowly.

I used to equate urgency with importance. Now, I find power in pause.

Day 11

Affirmation: Peace lives in the breath I haven't taken yet.

How to Implement: Pause right now and take three deep breaths—feel yourself soften.

In the middle of a stressful call, I stepped away to breathe. When I returned, I brought peace with me.

Day 12

Affirmation: I can feel deeply and still be grounded.

How to Implement: Let yourself cry today, but don't let the emotion carry you away.

I let the tears fall—but I didn't spiral. I stayed rooted. That was a new kind of power.

Day 13

Affirmation: I don't have to respond right away to be kind.

How to Implement: Delay one non-urgent reply until you're centered.

I used to reply instantly, even when I was overwhelmed. Now I respond when I'm ready—and that's more respectful to us both.

Day 14

Affirmation: Peace is a boundary, not a luxury.

How to Implement: Say no today in defense of your calm—not as a punishment, but as a gift to yourself.

I used to avoid conflict at the cost of my well-being. Now, my boundary is my peace treaty.

WEEK 3: December 15–21

Day 15

Affirmation: Peace doesn't mean the absence of struggle—it means I stay grounded in the storm.

How to Implement: Stay calm during one minor challenge today by grounding yourself.

When the chaos hit, I used to match its energy. Now, I meet it with breath and boundaries.

Day 16

Affirmation: I give myself permission to be soft in a world that expects me to be hard.

How to Implement: Respond to a tough moment today with softness instead of force.

I used to armor up every day. Now, I let softness protect me—it feels radical and freeing.

Day 17

Affirmation: I choose quiet over noise, even if others don't understand.

How to Implement: Decline one unnecessary conversation or interaction today.

I left the group chat on silent. My peace didn't ask for permission—it asked for space.

Day 18

Affirmation: I forgive not to forget—but to free myself.

How to Implement: Release one grudge you've been holding, even if silently.

I didn't call them. I didn't pretend it didn't hurt. I just stopped carrying the weight. That was my closure.

Day 19

Affirmation: I allow peace to exist in my body, not just in my mind.

How to Implement: Stretch, rest, or move today to invite peace into your physical space.

After years of holding tension in my shoulders, I exhaled so deeply it surprised me. My body finally felt safe.

Day 20

Affirmation: I release the urge to explain myself to people committed to misunderstanding me.

How to Implement: Choose not to defend yourself in one interaction where peace matters more than being right.

I let them think what they wanted. I walked away with my dignity intact—and my spirit unbothered.

Day 21

Affirmation: Peace grows when I honor the pace of my healing.

How to Implement: Do one thing slower than usual today—on purpose.

I used to rush through my mornings. Now I sip, breathe, and move like I'm worth the extra minutes.

WEEK 4: December 22–31

Day 22

Affirmation: I protect my peace as a sacred act of self-love.

How to Implement: Decline one energy-draining conversation or task today.

I used to say yes to stay liked. Now I say no to stay whole. My peace is my priority.

Day 23

Affirmation: I let go of emotional clutter that doesn't belong to me.

How to Implement: Write down what feelings are yours—and what you're carrying from others.

I walked around heavy for years until I realized half of it wasn't mine. Now I carry only what's true.

Day 24

Affirmation: I create peace by accepting what I cannot change.

How to Implement: Whisper to yourself today: 'It is what it is, and I am still okay.'

That thing I couldn't fix? I stopped trying. And suddenly, peace showed up where control used to live.

Day 25

Affirmation: I allow joy to coexist with healing.

How to Implement: Do something small today just because it makes you smile.

I used to think healing had to be serious. But I laughed so hard last night—and it felt like medicine.

Day 26

Affirmation: I choose peace even when others choose drama.

How to Implement: Walk away from one situation today instead of reacting.

They poked, waiting for me to explode. I smiled, stayed silent, and protected my peace instead.

Day 27

Affirmation: I deserve stillness, not just productivity.

How to Implement: Give yourself permission to rest—even if everything isn't finished.

The dishes weren't done, the email could wait. I chose peace over performance—and nothing fell apart.

Day 28

Affirmation: I don't need to chase closure to feel complete.

How to Implement: Write your own ending to something left open.

They never apologized. I never got a goodbye. But I wrote my own peace story—and it was enough.

Day 29

Affirmation: I forgive myself for the times I mistook chaos for connection.

How to Implement: Reflect on one lesson learned without blaming yourself.

I stayed too long because the noise felt familiar. Now I know silence can be safety too.

Day 30

Affirmation: Peace is the greatest gift I give to my future self.

How to Implement: Make one choice today your future self will thank you for.

I left that argument unread. I went to bed early. And tomorrow, I'll wake up lighter.

Day 31

Affirmation: I end this month in peace, not pieces.

How to Implement: Light a candle, play soft music, and close the month with intention.

I survived, I softened, I healed. This isn't just an ending—it's a sacred beginning.

ABOUT THE AUTHOR

Lynnette C. Anderson, M.S. is a Licensed Behavior Specialist, emotional intelligence educator, and founder of Think Instead. With over 20 years of experience working with individuals impacted by trauma, anger, and emotional overwhelm, she empowers women to reconnect with their truth and reclaim their voice.

Lynnette specializes in anger as a misunderstood emotion—one that often masks grief, guilt, fear, or deep unmet needs. Through her books, workshops, and healing spaces, she helps women stop apologizing for how they feel and start transforming that emotion into growth, boundaries, and bold decisions.

When she's not writing or leading transformational groups, you'll find her loving up on her grandchildren, journaling in quiet corners, or reminding women that their fire is sacred.

www.ingramcontent.com/pod-product-compliance
Lightning Source LLC
Chambersburg PA
CBHW072211070526
44585CB00015B/1285